T0351555

A PASSING BELL: GHAZALS FOR TINA

TINA KANE

A Passing Bell

Ghazals for Tina

Paul Kane

GEORGE BRAZILLER / NEW YORK

Copyright © 2019 by Paul Kane

Publication of this book has been supported by the Susan Turner Fund of Vassar College.

All rights reserved. No part of this publication may be reproduced or transmitted in any form by any means, electronic or mechanical, including print, photocopy, recording, or any other information and retrieval system, without prior consent of the publisher. Request for permission and reprint or to make copies, and for any other information, should be addressed to the publisher:

George Braziller, Inc.
90 Broad Street
New York, NY 10004

Library of Congress Cataloging-in-Publication Data

Names: Kane, Paul, 1950– author.
Title: A passing bell : ghazals for Tina / Paul Kane.
Description: First edition. | New York, NY : George Braziller, Inc., [2019]
Identifiers: LCCN 2018044197 | ISBN 9780807600252 (hardcover : alk. paper)
Subjects: LCSH: Ghazals, American.
Classification: LCC PS3561.A4715 A6 2019 | DDC 811/.54—dc23
LC record available at https://lccn.loc.gov/2018044197

First edition
Designed by Rita Lascaro
Printed in the United States of America

Contents

I shall find the dark grow luminous, the void fruitful when I understand I have nothing, that the ringers in the tower have appointed for the hymen of the soul a passing bell.

W. B. YEATS, *Per Amica Silentia Lunae*

Love is not a feeling. Love is put to the test, pain not. One does not say, "That was not true pain, or it would not have gone off so quickly."

LUDWIG WITTGENSTEIN, *Zettel*

Hafiz, if you so desire her presence, do not hide from Him: when you find your beloved, abandon the world—let it go.

HAFIZ, *Ghazals* 1

A Note on the Ghazal

.

The ghazal is a lyric poem common in classic Persian, Arabic, Turkish and Urdu poetry. Each line of the ghazal (called a bayt) has two parts and resembles a couplet. A unique feature of the form is that the last bayt usually contains the poet's name. The ghazal is often compared to the sonnet, in part because both are established lyric forms conventionally concerned with the vicissitudes of love. However, the ghazal in the hands of Sufi poets (including Hafiz, Attar and Rumi) evolved from an earthly love lyric into an expression of the mystic's love for God, though often in a veiled or allegorical way, where the poet's Beloved or spiritual Master is addressed.

PROLOGUE

·

This work began—and, yes, it is the work of mourning—on the flight home after his wife
   died unexpectedly, though everyone knew she had but a few months to live.

She wanted to go home, her true home in Australia, the home they had built there
   atop an old volcano in the goldfields. Unable to walk or speak, she could still command.

I went with them, of course. I've never been absent, even if he was only vaguely aware
   of my existence, inseparable from his. She, however, knew of me from the start.

And what a start! Startling, truly, as no one saw it coming, not even themselves, and no one
   approved, though that threw them together the more, having only each other.

But that is a different story. This follows on from that, and begins at the end, when she
   is gone, and he bereft, bewildered by loss, a loss so fundamental he is shocked to be alive.

·

He never meant to write this, it simply took shape and wouldn't let him go until it was over.
   But it will never be over for him, his heart inscribed with the name of his beloved, Tina.

GHAZAL 1

At night I lie awake and call to you,
      but you don't reply, except in silence.

The night bird is not silent but sings
      a simple single note. His mate does not sing back.

I do not understand this silence, as if God
      has departed and taken you with Him.

I have no words to form a prayer
      that could reach you or Him.

Two wine glasses sit on the counter top—
      one is full and then only half full.

Without emptiness the glass could not exist.
      If you should speak, Tina, the glass would shatter.

GHAZAL 2

We sat around and sang to you because
      you could not speak. Your eyes were your voice.

Fires burned all around to take off the chill.
      A different coldness was waiting for you.

I kissed your marble forehead when you left.
      The fire had gone out. What burned then?

You had the most eloquent hand.
      When you took mine, Heaven rang with joy.

Angels formed a circle, also hand in hand,
      to see the most delicate thing on Earth.

If flowers should weep, nectar would be tears,
      and the hummingbird would attend you, Tina.

GHAZAL 3

My words have already become extravagant
    because they do not know what to say.

I dress in the morning but my clothes don't fit.
    I must have lost weight or shrunk into myself.

When I stand at the window looking out
    the light changes everything as it changes.

A hill I hadn't noticed, a group of trees,
    cows on a hillside—how could I have overlooked them?

I cup my hands under the faucet to drink
    the cool water. If I persist, it is enough.

Summer was cruel to some of the trees you planted.
    They did not outlive you, Tina, nor have I.

GHAZAL 4

Whenever someone mentions your beauty
    my heart loosens and my breathing almost stops.

This is no way to live, but is there another way?
    Perhaps I take it all too seriously.

The last time you laughed, it was a surprise.
    I didn't know you could still do it.

Blessed be silliness. It's a portal to God.
    The last words you ever spoke were "I know, I know."

You know so much more now, everything
    we do not know and cannot yet.

Your lips are sealed. That is the way.
    But still I see your eyes, Tina, your eyes.

GHAZAL 5

Before we left on our trip, I planted new seeds
    so the garden would be flourishing on our return.

I have come back alone to tend the garden,
    but I won't be showing you what has grown.

Every night I brought in a basket of greens
    and placed them before you. You touched them lightly.

When I pressed my fingers to your soft ones,
    four wishes sprouted and one certainty.

None of the wishes came to pass, but we knew
    they wouldn't. We were certain about that.

In May, wildflowers—profuse—mock my diligence.
    Next spring, Tina, I think they will grow for you.

GHAZAL 6

When I came upon your poems, the ones
    I didn't know, you shone in a new light.

There are secrets hid in the shadows
    that only exist because of the light.

Shadows are the secrets the light keeps
    in order to reveal them when the time comes.

When the time came there were two quick breaths
    and I didn't catch what floated upon them.

God only knows what it all means.
    How could I have missed my one chance?

There is a new sound ringing in my ears.
    It sounds like your name, Tina, over and over.

GHAZAL 7

"My Beloved" I can only write. How say it aloud?
    Friends would scoff and enemies snicker.

My only wealth was your love—it made me worthy
    in my own eyes. Now I will have to learn to slink.

I will learn how to be a beggar, someone
    accepting of his worthlessness. My money is useless.

When we were poor and had only each other,
    we were despised. I don't blame people for it.

Even God turned away, though it was all His fault.
    Later, He let us come home and embraced us.

If I cry out from time to time, I hope
    you won't mind, Tina. It is God crying through me.

GHAZAL 8

If I were Hafiz or Ghalib, I would get drunk
    on wine, but I have only water in my home now.

I cut a poor figure of a poet, my obscurity
    well deserved. Thank God for my friends.

As for your friends, they are water rushing
    over a dam—their love impossible to detain.

I live in an oasis where the wells are drying up.
    Soon, I will have to venture out into the desert.

If this is fate, what does it mean? Shall I give
    myself over like the other poets and trust to love?

Your love I could trust. It never ran dry.
    But how, Tina, did you turn water into wine?

GHAZAL 9

Two sounds you hated: gunshots in the woods
      and the thud of a bird against a windowpane.

I could not protect you from either and grew
      to dread them too. Life is what mattered.

I think you were too sensitive for this world.
      You were born into the wrong one. It wronged you.

I know there is another world inside this one,
      but you have gone far away so there must be others.

There are certain stars that disappear when I look at them.
      Turn slightly aside and they reappear.

It's like that with you, Tina. Fixed at the center,
      but only visible at the periphery of my vision.

GHAZAL 10

Now that you're gone, I see the world through your eyes.
      You see through me—as you always did.

Now that I look for both of us, everything is doubled
      being halved, even though the parts don't add up.

I am ashamed to think of who I once was,
      drunk on the cheapest wine the bars served.

Now, what do I see? Your love of the pure act, innocence
      at the heart of what passes for simple.

This Coptic weaving, circular, radiant, is like that,
      a distillate fiery from a crucible of craft.

You knew that way of working, Tina, how—in your hands—
      the smallest thread could ravel up the world.

What is the good life, Master? To live without regret.
    Without regret? Who lives a good life?

The moon rises every night, longing for the earth,
    the earth longing for it. What separated them?

Tonight the moon, entangled in the trees, is orange and full.
    Death, I'm admonished, is part of life, like the inseparate moon.

When did you know you were dying? Before I did, before anyone.
    Who knew when you died? I only, my hand touching your face.

I died with you, of course, and have been dying since.
    How fortunate our ignorance. And our knowledge?

What is breath? What was that little sigh, Tina?
    Was it the sound of life turned inside out?

At night when the bats come out and clear the air,
    late summer sounds reverberate.

The ear is a shell full of noise, like hissing waves
    withdrawing from the shore. I listen for your name.

It has been forty days and you more boundless than before.
    I see no end in sight—darkness gathers in the trees.

It is time to say goodbye, but it's a word I cannot speak.
    It comes out of a language I never mastered.

When you lost utterly the power of speech, you spoke
    with new power, of hand and eye.

I am surrounded by silence, Tina, loud and discordant
    like the unseen chorus this summer eve.

For forty days I have worn the face of composure.
    It masks the heart, but fools no one.

For forty nights I have cowered in an intricate cave
    of memories and darker half-memories like dreams.

I live inside my life, or walk just behind it, the way
    you did with me on city streets—a gentle taunt.

For forty days a stranger in this desert, I stumble in the heat.
    Prone to mirage, I pant under thin bushes at noon.

Why am I an outcast? Will no one take me in?
    Am I so untouchable? Am I so touched?

Why didn't I listen to the prophecies, Tina?
    Because they were too true to believe.

When I failed to bring you home,
    I failed you.

I am held in disrepute now
    in the upper regions.

How can it not be right that
    I should suffer?

But death in life? There are no bounds
    to the truth.

In the town, people think me crazy,
    as do the angels.

You came home alone, Tina.
    And so did I.

GHAZAL 15

There came two kinds of comforters, those who needed
    comforting and those who missed the mark.

How could it be otherwise? They know only their own.
    How could they know the part wholly?

I made the same error myself. I grew
    to adjust for distortion, for pain.

Only those who stepped aside could see
    how unlikely you would happen again.

Only they could feel the lowering and lowering,
    the deep trough before a swelling wave.

It took me years sharing secrets, Tina, to know
    what I hadn't even known to wish to know.

GHAZAL 16

Cut your hand with a sharp kitchen knife,
    shock, blood and bone take all your mind.

Then pain—stinging, then throbbing—an agony to touch.
    At what point does the healing begin?

This wound isn't healing. It moves, seems to grow,
    taking on a coloration, a sharpening along the edges.

Time will heal. But if there is no time, only now,
    the blood doesn't clot, the ache aches.

In the late summer garden, morning glories proliferate
    strangling the roses, winding up, pulling them down.

Dear Tina, the garden's gone wild, with seed heads drooping
    in dismay, as if regret were a thorn under the skin.

When the Master called, I went in, finding him half blind.
    But he was already more myself than I.

Kneeling or bowing was out of the question: he stood holding
    one end of a table and asked me to take the other.

He said he needed my strength, and I believed it,
    though he knew I was among the weakest around him.

What he didn't say was that I would be unmade,
    that you'd make me again in the image of what I wasn't.

There would have to be fire, there would have to be change,
    with change bringing more fire, and fire suffering.

So, Tina, like clay modeled and bisqued, I entered the kiln,
    but later shattered, the shards strewn like scattered seed.

Make an error, apologize—it can almost wipe the slate.
    Make a fatal error, you cannot cast away remorse.

The trees grow beyond themselves, their branches threaten.
    Let in light, there is darkness in the shade, in shadows.

The shadows are darker than shade, they depend upon the light.
    Here, there is no light, except when I close my eyes.

There is a tree no bird will occupy to sing.
    This tree grows in a heaven abandoned by the gods.

If the gods were to speak, they couldn't utter a word. Words replaced
    them and they mouth syllables of who they once were.

In the minds—the hearts—of those who knew you, Tina,
    you're like a myth, casting shadows before us.

I am bound in time, wound in intricacies
    of the heart, the ties of earth.

If the Master speak truly, you're back of beyond,
    a land I've only glimpsed from the desert.

The impartial autumn moon glistens as if moist.
    It fills a void in the night sky.

Harvest Moon, red, lambent, why call me
    out of doors tonight, in the chill air?

Time is the homage God has chosen to pay Eternity.
    What concern is it of mine?

Tina, you live at an infinite extension
    that belies the death in my heart.

In the eclipse—the full moon a sliver of nebulous light—
    your studio lights unexpectedly shone, but I couldn't get inside

to turn them off. How came the door to be locked from inside?
    It was an eclipse of reason on a night of nights.

A ladder, an open window, sufficed to solve the problem, but
    not the mystery, compounded by a flash of light,

a beep of your stair lift, a power failure, as if—
    just in case—I hadn't quite got the message.

We have lived so long with explanations, we've forgotten
    the real questions we meant to pose.

"What is it, Tina?" I asked aloud. Then waited. But the moon
    had already begun to unfurl itself in the cold light.

By day I am solitary, at night lonely. Yet I'm not alone—
    dusk brings on the haunting, which comes in waves.

Under stars, years ago, the heavens a liquefaction,
    we looked up from that island as if underwater.

The island was an oasis of the sea, and we,
    we were stripped of all our belongings.

If emptiness above is mostly dark matter, the dark
    is as full as the ocean to its creatures.

I live behind a breakwater of piled boulders and debris,
    the edges sharp and ragged, not yet washed smooth.

Tropical storms out at a sea are driving high tides—
    when the surges come, Tina, I call them by your name.

With arms wrapped across my chest, I could be holding you
    and not my shattered heart. I might've smiled, not grimaced.

There are moments when I fear I'll lose this pain, but
    then, rueful, I laugh and know it cannot be.

All but the most stubborn leaves have fallen in cold rain—
    the gestural trees tender their barrenness to the sky.

Through the open woods, a slant of sun awakens a spectrum
    throwing itself against white walls and upon the red floor.

Dangling, the faceted prism hangs by a thread in the window seat,
    dismantling the sun into this rainbow.

White light sheared off and broken into all the colors of loss,
    while you, dear Tina, spin among motes like a photon.

Today our cohort from Italy gathered and lingered over lunch
    where you and I sometimes met your former boss—

though, really, you had no boss but yourself, a taskmaster
    inspiriting you as if nothing could be more serious

than joy, nothing more intimate than conscience.
    You, the conductor, always knew the score.

At the end, people thought you'd changed but, no,
    they saw who you were when they weren't around.

It is November now, and time has given up on solace,
    so we have each other again, at long last.

Those knew you best who knew you least, and last, because
    by then, Tina, you were moving out of time, into love.

A full moon at Christmas, five months on, and two days after
    your friends sang to you again as they did that last week.

The moon rises slowly, slower than the sun setting, though
    not as slow as the night falling and the constellations turning.

I'm back in Australia, at the outer edge of our world—
    an edge you slipped off of in a matter of minutes.

Solitude's not loneliness nor loneliness solitary—
    I share it with you when you are present.

Master, you said take nothing on faith. We believed that.
    Master, I am not faithless, I believe in these vows.

Tina, in singing to you again, the notes were like the tears
    blearing the moon rising in the east, full, radiant.

There is a large orange hole low in the sky—
    perhaps it is the eye of God come to this remote place.

But now it is hooded, as if an eyelid closing with its flap of skin.
    Bands of cloud are faintly illumined,

the flush embers of a fire dying out.
    I am left with wind—testing the windows for weakness—

and sudden darkness, the moon held at bay.
    The eye reappears above the blindfold,

unblinking, an aperture wide open. And then
    it is gone in the unzipping of night.

The sky is a shell: the sun, moon, and stars pierce it.
    But that's just a passing fancy, Tina, a whistling in the dark.

Tomorrow this terrible year will end and the first year begin
    that you will not see since the day you were born.

We didn't celebrate last year either, asleep in a hotel in Auckland,
    not knowing your last year already upon us.

And what if we had known? We knew all we needed to know.
    I wish we had known less. Ignorance failed us.

When the Master said, "Think upon your death," we did.
    It was nothing like what we imagined.

Master, why didn't you tell us the sky's dome would shatter
    around us, that we would walk on pieces of glass?

For months I've tried to reassemble the shards, careless of the cuts.
    Tina, when I fall to pieces, it's because you are there whole.

As the storm blew in, prismatic light shone, flat and horizontal.
    Then—just now—a vertical rainbow appeared.

Or rather, a few shards of color, orange and green,
    fading into undifferentiated gray clouds.

Every sunset here belongs to you—they need not be dramatic.
    The end of the day is not the end of day.

Morning comes early. It wakes me and then I begin to awaken.
    That's when the day starts, when I'm beyond myself.

At that moment, I greet you, though you have been waiting
    all night—or so it seems when the mirror glimpses me.

If I watch the sunset and forget myself in remembering,
    it is the world, Tina, that moves, not the sun.

You almost died in this house on the high hill—
    we got you to the hospital instead, not anticipating death.

I stopped in front of it the other day to stare at it again.
    It's just brick and glass and a thousand torn lives.

What I saw was myself instead, and you in memory
    of that night—no, that morning—when I still had hope.

I've given up on hope. Or perhaps it's given up on me.
    Inside is so often outside these days, these nights.

I passed a slow-moving herd of cattle today on the back road,
    their flat foreheads and flat hinds a kind of fate.

How you flung your heart out to animals, Tina!
    Their pure vulnerability, their fatal being!

Each of the thirty hills we look out upon from our deck
    is a story known only to us, so personal our viewpoint.

Of course I say we and us—that hasn't changed in the change.
    I built this house for you, every nail driven home and clinched.

How can this not be ours, how can the landscape not be endowed?
    A plume of smoke in the distance, a grass fire no doubt.

Nothing is drier than the Victorian bush in summer: it burns.
    We fled fire once, then next year floods, followed by locusts.

Light and shadow was all the world you wanted up here.
    That, and the enormous sky embracing everything.

I remember the night when a comet took up a quadrant of the sky.
    It silenced us, Tina, in showing a scale we intuited as ours.

What does it mean to say I'm back? Did I even leave?
    It's just a gap in time, and might as well be a dream, though it wasn't.

I've no time for regrets: I'm too busy visualizing what went wrong.
    Was there a trigger, an event, something avoidable?

This is the gap I live in. Travel accentuates it, as exhaustion does an illness.
    I'm back to where I began: it's all a circle, a cipher, a zero.

I took you with me halfway round the world, then back.
    How well you endured it! It was unbearable otherwise.

Everyone I meet reminds me of you, whether they mean to or not.
    You remind them of the gap that has opened up.

Dear Tina, people are still finding out you're not here,
    not knowing how present you remain—and how ghostly.

It's 10:01 pm, January twenty-fourth, North America,
    exactly six months later, to the minute.

To those outside of it, what can time be? The same
    as here, where now is only now?

I live and die in the past and the future. And yet,
    I cannot measure the duration of a single breath.

You brought a snowstorm last night, and hours of morning work.
    How labor intrigued you, the physicality of force!

Force over Distance equals Work, a displacement you lived by.
    Your duty was to yourself—which was larger than you.

Tina, what can I say at this moment? At one minute
    after twelve, in real time, you left time behind.

O, Master, when you spoke to her that evening while others listened
    it was as if thoughts fluttered dove-white above us.

We could not comprehend the conversation, but knew it to be
    for us, if only later, when we would understand.

Light and lightness came together then to illumine the room,
    but there was heat and power, too, which surely you intended.

She said she was shocked by what she saw in herself,
    and you said she was swimming out of sight of two shores.

From this shore to that farther one is a lifetime and then some—
    not everyone makes it, but she did: we saw her wade ashore.

I think you are swimming still, Tina, but across another bay
    extending out to a very different sea from the one I stand beside.

When your friends from the city came up to lay flowers on your grave,
 the scene seemed bleaker than what I see, visiting every day.

Alone, I am enveloped by presence—or absence—and the moment comes alive.
 With others, the plainness of a plot of ground cleaves to the ordinary.

The winter has not been hard so far, if we stick to weather talk.
 I don't have words for what I've weathered, or haven't.

Five deer ran across the yard tonight, startled by my sudden appearing.
 They have not heard the news that the female has disappeared.

The deer are too nervous to stop and listen to the chittering birds,
 who, like your friends from the city, could say a lot about you.

People come and go, call, write and then fall silent, but every night,
 Tina, I hear your voice, and every day I offer mine.

We sold that house today, the one not ours, the family get-away,
 a place you would never call home nor feel at home in,

but a place of memories nonetheless, sometimes memorable,
 as when you first came, before we were together, a visitor.

There's a watercolor of yours framed on the wall there.
 Shall I leave it for the new owners or try to get it back?

These are idle thoughts. Nostalgia is like a strip of gauze
 over seeping memories that won't properly heal.

Everywhere I look there's blood, dried and crusted,
 the granules of life impotent, inert.

The weather has turned cold, Tina, bitter with a biting wind
 that roars in my ears, stinging my watering eyes.

St. Valentine's Day: a homemade card and dining out was ritual,
    even in your last year, minus the food.

By then I was a nurse and you, you were like a pagan goddess:
    the world came to you and you blessed it in your embrace.

I would count my blessings now if I could find them.
    I search for them every day at your graveside.

It's below zero now, just the right temperature for grief.
    I left flowers today. Perhaps they will freeze and stay fresh.

I listened to your recorded voice in conversation with the Master.
    Only now do I understand what it all meant.

We measure distance in light years now, and as for time,
    well, you didn't run out of time, Tina, you outran it.

I'm inundated by memories but why are so few happy?
    My distracted gaze falls upon objects that light up darkly.

Not a thing that doesn't carry imbedded pain,
    be it of loss, accident, disability, poignancy.

Every accomplishment, no matter how small, was once a victory:
    ashes, clinkers in the coal grate when the fire failed.

Last week it was so cold the drain pipes froze.
    Everything seems harder in winter, taxing takes its toll.

I am not cut out for this life, there must be some mistake—
    something's not right. Can we go back and try it again?

O, Master, you endured beyond endurance, and Tina,
    you endured all until your body could endure no more.

When thunder came and the sky lit up in sheets of light,
    it was your death day, seven months on, or off.

Weathering these weather events I associate with you
    is inner weather, deeply mine and superstitious.

I don't believe in my beliefs but I act as though I do.
    How else make sense of what doesn't make any sense?

You should be alive. You should be sitting in your chair
    reading a letter from Christine or a book from the Met.

I don't know why you're not there. Do you?
    O, Master, if you were alive you would tell me.

Fourteen thousand miles away, Aboriginal lightning snakes
    await you, Tina, wrapped around your funeral pole.

When he took his life, his spouse cried out your name,
    the very opposite of the decision to die.

You refused death in accepting all that it brought you.
    You would not die, though in the end your body did.

I would not let you die, though powerless to stop it—
    we lived as if tomorrow were today every day of the week.

Some thought this brave, others questionable, but to us
    it was simply a question of life, and life was the answer.

I am out of answers now, and have only questions.
    The simplest are the hardest. Why am I alive?

I am become an old man, bent like a question mark.
    O, Tina! I exclaim, trying to unbend.

O, Master, are you the muse of these lamentations?
    Where are they going? Where am I, now that my life is over?

This is endless sorrow, the more so in fixing it in verse.
    Perhaps oblivion will overtake us both, my poems and me.

Is that what you have in mind, Master? Speaking beyond the grave?
    I look upon the scratchy sod and see nothing but it.

I look at the sky. I see the sun. I look at the underside of eyelids,
    I see nothing, not even darkness. I see my mind.

With what do I see, Master? Not even an angel can see me
    for what I am. Master, you gave me my eyes

when Tina became my seeing. At last, I saw the world.
    O, Master, do you believe your eyes?

I live by words whose purpose is to say what cannot be said—
    I call it poetry but that is merely a word.

Alone, lonely, solitary, solitude, the reality slips between
    like the undulating force we see as waves on the shore.

Today is my natal day. Again I set out upon the sea.
    The tide will carry me away and, if I survive, bring me back.

I wish these metaphors weren't true, that I might control them.
    The opposite is the case. I wish it were just a matter of language.

I wish we had a language for what is real. We could call it intuition.
    Another word. But out of all the languages you spoke,

Tina, this was the one everyone heard behind the words.
    Call it eloquence. Call it silence. Call it...

A calendar coincidence, Good Friday, your mother's death day
    and yours together, as her ashes lie with you in your coffin.

I have spent the day revolving around twin foci,
    an ellipse that has left me dizzy and breathless.

How long can this go on before emptiness turns to fullness,
    absence to presence, grief to joyful remembrance?

When will this dark song turn back and all the sunlight of your being shine?
    Could I even stand the brilliance, as if emerging from a cave?

Everyone looks askance, to see if I have returned from the underworld.
    How could I not look back, when I can't look forward?

I will say nothing of suffering on this day of days, which belongs
    to you, Tina, and to your mother, whom I also loved.

And now it is nine months with the weight of accumulated days
    like a pressure on the chest when you're close to tears.

Spring has returned and the world is growing again,
    the sky dilates, the air freshens, the grass greens.

If I said my heart had blackened to a lump of coal,
    you would say toss it in the fire to burn and flame out.

But, no, you wouldn't say that, nor would I.
    No one talks like that. And I barely talk at all.

What happens to me is of so little account thinking of what will happen
    when I'm no longer me but a life unbound seeking some light.

I hope the light will be yours, Tina, though that is a vain hope since
    you suffuse me already. You can't be the sun and the sky, can you?

Last night thunder woke me out of a sleep I thought
    a waking, so strong my dreams of you have become.

I did not hear it rain for the downpour within me,
    but thunder cannot be denied, and in spring I welcome it.

The grass will be greener today under a pale white sky.
    This world of mine within the world will be more relaxed

after the intensities of the blue and dazzling light. Already,
    my breathing is deeper, my sadness part of the landscape.

The little stream behind the barn flows nowhere in particular,
    losing itself in the far fields of black dirt, mixing with the earth.

Every day I visit your grave as if I visit you, Tina,
    but every day it is you who visits me like this rain.

O Master, forgive me my weakness, which unmans me in grief,
    and forgive me my strength, which denies you daily.

I know how much work I have yet to do, walking stiffly along the road
    leading away from the house that was once a home.

Homeless in spirit and rich in possessions, I am leaving everything behind
    except the wind which blows constantly on this hard-packed dirt.

Where am I? Dusk is falling and the dew seems to rise around me.
    Is this solitude the last gift I will ever receive in gratitude?

No, this track turns familiar, I recognize it now for what it is
    and where it goes. For all its twistings, it takes me back where I began.

This is delirium, Tina, and I should know it by now. It is what
    our Master warned against even as he set us upon this road.

When the angel came to me I didn't recognize him,
    his wings were hidden, he seemed like anyone else

who had known you, coming to say consoling words. But behind
    the words a great space opened out and I was standing

in a shimmering place where the wind was visible like waves.
    It was very quiet and what the angel said deepened the silence.

I have forgotten his words and recall only what they meant, that you
    were living in a foreign land and I must travel to find it.

But first, I need to learn the language of that place, its
    grammar of absence, its self-erasing syntax, voiceless verbs.

I'm afraid it will take me the rest of my life, Tina, so please
    be patient, don't wander away to where I can't find you.

My poems cry out when I start to write them down,
    "Why do you make us come into being like this?"

They are like newborns shocked by the harsh alien air
    or fish gasping at the bottom of a boat from what gives us life.

My poems are part of a larger life which includes death, naturally,
    but only because, for them, death is another kind of life.

But I will not speak out against this language of mine. Poor as it is,
    it is all I have to conjure a semblance of you.

When I Work, there comes a moment when I enter your world and,
    though it is dark, I sense a movement as if wings fluttered nearby.

That's when I bring the poem back, drawing it after me,
    for it has touched you, Tina, and I cannot let it go.

For two days I was verging on tears, an embankment
    I tried not to slide down for I knew what lay at the bottom,

a ditch that drained the road above, full of leaves and marshy mud,
    old bottles and rusty cans, stuff thrown from passing cars.

I know I am drawn to edges, just as I am to roofs and lookouts.
    Fearlessness is just another form of fear, one you embrace.

For two days I sorted the artwork you left behind
    and the images that each called forth of a time and place, or

should I say placelessness and timelessness? I have no
    memory without you, as my life only began with you.

If I was no one before I was with you, Tina, who
    am I now, now that you are gone? You took me with you.

You have become all my knowledge and all my feelings.
    I buy cut flowers obsessively, as if their beauty were yours.

In every room they speak of you, knowingly, feelingly.
    Now that it is truly Spring I stand at the bottom of the stairs

outside and wait for all the colors to reach me: each green
    richer by the day and every day bringing new flowerings.

So why, last night, did I dream you took your own life?
    I was inconsolable and blamed myself, but when you explained

how you did it, simply falling headfirst off a marble plaza,
    you were alive to say so, for even dreams have a logic.

Of course I woke up then, or I might have died too. But tell me,
    Tina, what am I to say to friends who ask me how I am?

When I closed your eyes my hands swept across your brow
    like a benediction or the last rites of a church of two.

It was then I began to see the world through your eyes, as if seeing
    for the first time how truth marries compassion,

and that, sundered from you, I no longer mattered to myself
    in the same way, but stepped aside to let others pass.

I found myself standing on the curb, watching how everyone reflected
    some aspect of you: a smile, a frown, concern, simple happiness.

Why could I not see it before? You pointed it out to me every day,
    and daily my eyes were unseeing as if in sleep-walking.

When I kissed your brow, already growing chill, my lips burned
    with shame, Tina, that you should have to die for both of us.

Now that the leaves are back, as if migrating birds
    always returning to the same sacred spot—

though who knows what is sacred to birds or trees?—
    the morning light has finally something to play with,

shining and dazzling toys which the wind makes a game of.
    And those birds that came back, and the ones that stayed all winter,

they are at their games, too, and their songs of attraction.
    May is the month when the world turns over—*our* world,

I was going to say, but then I'll say it anyway—our world
    that we share every morning in a ritual not so much

of remembering as of sensing rhythms of blood and breath,
    as you return, Tina, as I turn towards you.

The flowers—carnations—in the vase next to your photograph
    are the same color as the lilacs outside the window.

The birds—blue jays—flitting among branches—move
    with the same motion as impressions of you in my mind.

But they are not the same. Nothing's the same. I'm not happy
    when reminded of you, only when I remind others.

Then you are like these flowers and birds, though unlike them too.
    After all, nothing can be the same, even if everything

is embraced by light, as by shadows which are married to light.
    If there is darkness within me, it is like an undeveloped negative.

Dear Tina, I write these letters—these words—in the morning or
    at night because in between is the empty arc of my life.

O Master, we lived long enough that, like the Psalmist's,
    our foes were confounded, our enemies confused by our love,

dispersed, scattered abroad. But then we discovered them within—
    devious, intractable, all the more potent for being hidden.

We could not cry out, O Lord smite them down,
    for they were us and already held the citadel.

It took us a long time to come to terms with them,
    their demands never-ending, their intelligence about us complete.

In the end we had to give up, surrendering our illusions
    paraded before us as if captives in a Roman triumph.

But you took the lead, Tina, and one by one slowly converted
    these foes into believers in truth, which does not die.

It was a steep climb and there was no path but the one we made among
    boulders and shrub, the footing loose and we not wholly prepared.

I can see it in my mind now, though perhaps I have conflated
    several climbs during that terrible time when we only had each other,

when all we had was all we really wanted.
    But still, the climb wound higher and winded us.

I know the sun shone, but did it feel hot or was it like the clarity of cold?
    I know that when we reached the pass, it was in shadow.

Each step had a fatality about it. You couldn't think beyond it.
    You just kept going, not knowing, not hoping, just moving.

Tina, I have become confused about which climb this is. There was
    a mountain pass, we went through it and came out the other side.

O Master, have you turned away from me because this sorrow
    has taken your place? The heart has more than one chamber.

It is ten months to the day since that day, which has never ended.
    I live it over every day, for my time forward has stopped.

Every day I go out of my house alone to face the day. There is
    a sun, too bright to look at, a sky too high to touch.

There are creatures who regard me and run or flit away. There are
    people who no longer dare ask me how I'm doing.

And yet I live another life, too, full of encounters and smiles.
    It is not unreal, though it may seem a mask or a forgetfulness.

It is just life living through me. I no more control it, Tina,
    than the cells in my body that heal a cut—because they must.

I traveled, a modern pilgrim, to a place you called your own,
    O Master. You were there, though not there, veiled like love after death.

The tall trees made their presence felt—they have seen it all,
    though blind. I no longer know what knowing is, if not a feeling.

I met kindness. He was a simple man, not poor, not rich, earnest.
    He did not know the platitudes, just words washed in suffering.

I know we are misguided, Master, but there is no other way forward.
    The trees stand and sway. What is it to them if we fail or almost succeed?

When I came back, every object I touched, touched me in return.
    Every object a memory, every memory an object I hold or let fall.

There are shatterings all around me, Tina, and though I sweep them up,
    I make no headway. My new life could not be simpler. But it must.

What words are these that well up like tears not shed?
    Is it not enough just to be, without recording having been?

Is it an image you seek? The wild rose entangles the lilac bush
    and flowers in secret. Won't that do, for love or sorrow or nature's way?

Take it and leave me—I have too much to do today to truck
    with words or sit in shadows or even sunlight.

Entanglement is all the rage. The more I try to be alone,
    the more public my grief. There's no getting away or to.

Words are a kind of solitude when I speak them aloud,
    mostly to you, my only audience, sole auditor, or so I imagine.

When I call out to the dead, do they come round to listen?
    Tell me, Tina, do words travel faster than the speed of sound?

I woke to a moan that was exactly the pitch of your voice
      when caught in a nightmare. This was my nightmare come to accuse me.

"To live so far beneath the sky with the weight of a ruined life"—
      a line I wrote years ago that has come back now as a haunting.

Were "if only" an "as if," I could remake time in the image of sanctity.
      For what was sacred to me was the joy of sparking joy in you.

But who are you now? I have no concept of it, living in "if only."
      When I am turned around and face your absence, I am in your presence.

"Only if" becomes my way, as if a maze turned out to be only a labyrinth
      with you at the heart of it. Only if my work is mine is it yours too.

I do not forget that voice in the small hours of the night, Tina:
      I hear it and know I must live with it, if ever I'm to wake from this sleep.

I'm surrounded by the things I gave you, many gifts over many years,
      but none of them have outlived you, for they are perishable.

You have even outlived yourself, leaving behind a history, a person knowable.
      I know you now in the way you are unknowable, untethered.

I buy flowers weekly, creating what must look like little shrines.
      But they're not. They're just reminders that beauty has to be taken in.

The gardens, now in gorgeous bloom, are also reminders
      that beauty is work, and work beauty when the body blooms.

Cut flowers wilt, the perennials disappear, disturbed soil sprouts weeds.
      Books, prints, handmade cards, bits of jewelry attract dust, like to like.

How you used to give things away so easily, Tina, freely
      acknowledging that they were nothing to you, as if nothing were everything.

A cooling breeze blew through the open window this morning
    in our bedroom. It seemed freshness itself, this first day of summer.

This first summer without you—my life before you was not yet my life,
    just as my life after you is simply another space I have to fill.

What will I fill this day with, a day so perfect and poised?
    It is like an image of serenity—so often mistaken for sorrow.

Or is it the other way around? I have lost my bearings, the first step
    in getting lost altogether. But wherever I turn I find you, a homing.

Spring seemed long this year, even as I cannot account for the hours.
    The clock makes meaningless clicks which I register as time passing.

I think in seasons now—I cannot bear years or months, weeks or days.
    Each hour is a season without you, Tina, or an open window with a breeze.

I would like to sing a song of love on this, our anniversary day.
    Thirty-six years ago, on the steps of Firefly House, a small gathering.

Early morning—we had wanted dawn but the J.P. wouldn't do it—
    early days, with the promise of so many to come and go.

O Master, your wife blessed us from her sickbed, older than her years.
    "Be good to each other," is all she said, except for her smile and a nod.

It was your house, after all, and we wouldn't have been there but for you.
    But this is a reminiscence, not a song—where is the joy?

I cannot sing such a song right now, a fledgling abandoned
    and deaf to all the music around it in caroling June.

I want to say, Tina, that love is music, but you would scoff:
    love is the ground tone out of which music arises, falls, rises.

Not my hopes for you—that all you undertook go well, workaday,
    friendships, disputes, travels, inner working—*but you.*

Not my fears for you—that, overburdened, you would lose your balance,
    fall and be hurt by those who did not wish you well—*but you.*

Not my ideas about you—that you were a certain way because
    that is how I saw you through the prism of desire—*but you.*

Not my dreams about you—that you were other than who you were
    and that somehow I must be different too in that light—*but you.*

Not my expectations of you—that who you were would remain that way,
    unchanged, without the surprise of a sudden transforming—*but you.*

Not my version of who you were, Tina—which was always impoverished
    beside the enriching realness of every day together—*but you.*

It happened. We knew it would, just not on this day
    a year ago within hours of your holding her hand in silence.

It was time for my mother to leave—this she believed or knew.
    We could not have held on to her any more than you could that night,

which became the next day, and that day the end which doesn't end,
    or hasn't, the prelude to your last day exactly a month later.

How easy it is to tell a story—a matter of sequence and drama,
    as if the pattern of everything around us revealed itself transparently.

Light is retrospective, retroactive. The sun does not light our days,
    which are as dark to us in living them as our dreams at night.

This day happened, Tina, and I live with it still, like a shadow
    behind the shadow that the light of the past casts forward.

Last night I sat in the midst of music, as it filled a cathedral.
    So much contemplating of sorrow and suffering by way of beauty.

Why should what we create be so sad when joy is at the heart of it all?
    There must be something true in it, so obvious I can't see it.

How I hate subtlety when it's only a mask for emptiness.
    Give me pure emptiness. I will fill it brimful with my own.

Today, eleven months after, I fear only the forgetting that comes
    not with time but with the slow closing of a wound, as on a tree,

a bulge and roughness of the bark the sole sign of having been hurt.
    I do not want pain, but I will take suffering as if it were music.

Tina, you would have been in your element here: the finer
    the vibration, the more it resonated, the music of you.

What if you had never been? What would I be or have been?
    I would not exist. Someone with my name would walk the earth.

Someone who never got the chance to step out of the current of his life
    would be carried along still, just as he was meant to be.

I do not know what was meant to be, but I know what wasn't:
    the waste of life in all the approved forms of our sleepwalking.

There are dreams, there are nightmares. I am intimate with both:
    they shadow me, and often I turn towards them as if to embrace.

And then there is the sun, searingly bright and indifferent,
    like someone true to himself, the needle always pointing north.

Is it you I am talking about, Tina? Yes and no, like all metaphor.
    I think of your warmth, and how everyone around you felt it too.

In these poems you exist and I exist. We are free.
 In these poems, the landscape holding us has no horizon.

I know what freedom is, for I have tasted it in all its sweetness.
 When it comes to me, it is not mine but it is me.

And I have had enough to detect its bitterness, too, its aftertaste.
 That is why it is necessary to write these poems recording its passage.

If this imagined world weren't true, neither of us would be here,
 and no one would know that you and I were still together.

Our secret is out. But that's just a turn of phrase, since
 our privacy was so public and what we shared so visible.

Summer has stood still, it seems, just for a moment, as if pausing
 the way you used to, Tina, before saying something that was on your heart.

Those days of happiness that brought tears to our eyes,
 sheer exuberance of living in the light of the sun,

the sun another name for what burned within us by day
 and shone as a field of stars at night against the dark.

Days of tears are like moments in a life distilled to salt,
 irrigated soil that turns barren and encrusted over time,

the fruited trees and vines tough and small like hard memories.
 We try to wipe away those tears, each a shooting star.

It is so easy to confuse which tears are which, joy or sorrow,
 since they taste the same should we kiss them away.

Why should we turn away from what is tender in our lives?
 Dear Tina, at night in your arms, sun and stars dissolved.

I have a secret, known only to me and to you ever since that day
    you showed me your thumbnail, the way it had suddenly blossomed.

Your hands were flowers that day and I gathered them like a bouquet
    and put them to my lips and took in their sharp fragrance.

My secret was bound up in your hands, it was truly in your hands.
    I've never told anyone and no one but you has known how to read my heart.

I would give my heart away if I knew how and someone wanted it.
    But it wouldn't be a real gift since it would be hollowed out.

Better to hold on to it amidst the clutter of my life, the books,
    papers, correspondence, the useless magazines and journals.

If someone were to peer into my life, what would they see?
    They would not see you, Tina, the one person who knows my secret.

How do I know you don't know more about life, being dead?
    Perhaps it appears a multicolored slick on a pool of water, like oil,

an iridescence in the light, ever-moving, floating above the depths below,
    unaware of what lies under the surface? Or perhaps it's like

a long Gothic tapestry wound on an ancient wooden loom, each day
    lines of weft building up scene after scene in a woven tabernacle of years?

Perhaps our lives here seem unreal, as poets so often contend, as if
    holograms or insubstantial wavering images, mirages in the heat?

I would think it very sad to watch the terrible goings-on, the tragedies,
    but perhaps they, too, seem unreal, unbounded by time or space?

If I know anything, Tina, it is that I am bound to this world and
    to you, even if you are free, as I hope one day to be.

Today I leave and travel over an ocean I will not see.
    There is no ocean larger or more meaningful to me for what it holds.

If I said it holds memories that wouldn't be true, for it is motion itself
    and memories are like coral reefs, some rich with life, others bleached.

I will travel this ocean at a great height and in darkness for a day.
    Two score times we will have done this, for I take you with me.

O Master, will you come too? Or will you already be there waiting
    when I step into the cold morning air of another world, blinking at light?

Today I leave just as a year ago we left, thinking we would return.
    But we didn't. That is the entirety of my story: we never came back.

I came back alone, an integer of heartbreak, a solitary sorrow.
    Tina, when you returned it wasn't you, for you were already waiting here.

I arrived a few days before you and waited until you came.
    I don't know why that should have happened, but here we are now.

Two glorious days of sun and stillness, then this fog and dampness.
    I can see nothing but a milky sameness in all directions, a cloud.

To go from solitude to seclusion could be a comfort, if I could be comforted.
    The cloud is upon my skin, its moisture pervasive, enveloping.

This is like turning inward in the quietest moment of the evening
    when there is nothing left of day and the night doesn't yet know itself.

Do I know myself in this blank realm of eclipse? It is what I am
    mostly when I am unaware of the cloud unawareness.

If that seems too abstract, it's not so much an abstraction as an acknowledgment
    that, like you, Tina, we are more than we are, know it or not.

At daybreak the ragged tips of the cloudbank obscuring the sunrise
      burn with the intensity of a lamp wick trimmed to its lowest point.

No passion could possibly burn brighter, though I have been
      that incandescent flame and know what it consumes.

The sun is a violence and we live and perish in a violent world.
      Even peace must be fought for if it is to become another sun.

To be human is to be aflame, a self-immolation, a pyre.
      There are days when I doubt I have sufficient fuel.

Those are the days I am most human, a backlit cloud delaying dawn.
      What can I honestly say about my prospects when my life is mostly over?

I am back in the country of your country, Tina, a spirit land that has
      claimed me because I gave it my heart when you gave me yours.

The road I walk is one of sadness. I scuffle its crushed brown gravel.
      Every time I lift a foot, I defy the fact that I am bound to this earth.

Every time my step falls upon the road, I admit my bondage. I am not
      free like you. Whatever form you have taken, it is unimaginable.

Perhaps it is a place, a placeless place, or something more like dark energy,
      which is why you penetrate me as if I were air or emptiness.

Today our mountain is once again in fog, invisible to those living in the lowlands.
      Earlier, Mt. Beckworth floated above this sea of cloud that has arisen.

It is very still. The grass and bushes still visible seem to be waiting.
      For what, I could not say. But then, they are not waiting. I am.

For what, I think I know. It is time to go now, to start walking again.
      There is a day approaching, Tina, that will only come if I go out to meet it.

Our love was always a response to the anguish of the world.
  We felt it in our bones and like marrow it nourished us.

That is why you collected stones wherever we went and took them home.
  You inclined to the hard, which has its own beauty. The real you loved.

How could the end not be hard? How could our anguish not be beautiful?
  In those final days you were as radiant as on our wedding day.

O Master, why did you give us such an appetite? Why this food?
  Was it to offset the joy we felt, to balance our accounts?

Or was it to deepen the joy by marrying it to sorrows? If so,
  it has worked. I cannot pick up a stone now without testing its weight.

There are tears that weigh more than a stone and anguish as light as air.
  When my day comes, Tina, I want you by my side.

For the life of me, I did not believe you would die that day we drove
  through the night to the hospital, the ambulance silent, I following.

The longest day of my life and yours, without sleep and not yet without hope.
  Holding hands, you held on as I held you, all our years distilled to waiting.

And your body doing what the body does, fighting off infection, surviving,
  surviving right to the end, that next morning, when it began to die.

The body knows how to die. It follows a script as in a sacred ceremony.
  But somehow I have gotten ahead of myself: this is not the day you died.

This is the day you tried to live, rallying and squeezing my hand.
  All the machines said you would live, their numbers arcing upwards.

This was the last day of our lives together, Tina, for we lived on hope,
  which was like a foreknowledge of what would come to pass.

Today is your memorial. Did you remember? Can I help you remember?
  I could tell the minutes of this day as if it were yesterday or tomorrow.

A day that began as a problem to be solved with patience and care.
  And then I was slammed up against a wall, the terrible certainty

that you would die. The monitors turned off, the lights dimmed, the door shut.
  Just you and me waiting together for the end, that faintest of sighs

as if your body released your spirit with regret and reluctance,
  knowing it couldn't have it back and couldn't live without it.

I know how it felt. I feel it every day, since today is every day.
  I will bury you again at noon, a little ceremony of my own.

Just you and me, Tina, in the privacy of our love, in the embrace—
  that final embrace!—of release, upon which we based our love.

The man from the morgue who came to collect you in your green bag
  balked when he saw me still sitting by your side in the darkened room.

The nurses reassured him and I looked on as they put you in a box
  and wheeled you off down the corridor to the cold basement.

That was the beginning of loneliness, though it didn't strike me right away.
  The business of death is all-consuming. The emptiness bides its time.

Last night I woke up to a square of moonlight on the bedroom floor.
  There was an icy wind blowing the stars across the clear sky.

Now, this morning, we are fogged in, sitting inside a cloud.
  It will burn off and patches of blue will appear, faintly at first.

That's the way a day like today goes, when you are alone with it.
  I will be reliving each day now, Tina, as looking back is looking forward.

Everywhere I go, people speak of you as if a breath of being.
    We have drunk wine of astonishment and know our helplessness.

You have taught us that, though not you alone: it is part of our being.
    How often some of us have stopped and wished to ask you something.

I ask it still and wait for the answer to come to me as if my own.
    Perhaps it is. Perhaps you have taken up residence within me.

What should we build now together? We were always building something.
    Can two people compose a single soul? Were we ever separate in that sense?

When you lay next to me at night, whose breathing was whose?
    Did one inhale and the other exhale? Certainly our bodies knew no boundaries.

When I would lift you from your chair, pivot, and carry you, Tina,
    we could not have been closer, knowing every day was closer to the last.

When I turn off the bedside lamp at last and say good night,
    it is the silence I am addressing since it is so palpably there beside me.

When I stand by your grave and tell you what has happened this day,
    I speak to an absence that can never be truly done away with.

When I find myself sighing, murmuring your name over and over,
    it is not you I am thinking of but the ghost who has taken your place.

When someone speaks of you in my presence and I nod knowingly and smile,
    there is no breath in my body but a vacuum that has sealed my lungs.

Take today, for instance, the last morning I'll spend on our mountain—
    am I not gone already, and hasn't that departure been waiting here all along?

Of course I'll be back, Tina, if it is within my power, and so will you,
    as if two negatives could make a positive, and a positive a life.

Now that I have returned to our other home, north to the other south,
    and have traversed the hemisphere and clawed back a day I'd lost,

I realize that you have become my solitude, since I find you here
    as well as there, as naturally as day slides into the bell of night.

There is no flight that I could take that would separate us now.
    At every check point you are there as they screen me and our belongings.

At night, in the heat of this summer, I am naked sleeping beside you.
    If I reach for you, you are there, warm as the memory of our first embrace.

I have become transparent to myself, my guile as laughable as a child's.
    You have done this to me, you and the Master of who we are.

There is no respite from the heat this morning, so I will treat it as
    you might, Tina: soft, delicious, a kindness, a welcome home.

In the end there was only the look in your eyes, which said everything
    that needed to be said between us, as if words had only ever been a kind of looking.

In the end, it only took a certain glance my way for me to understand
    whatever it was you needed at that moment, in that particular place.

A chair, a couch, a bed were stations of the cross in a daily service,
    and movement forward was circular, like the telling of beads.

That I worshipped you was never in question, though you questioned it.
    You knew too much to let ignorance pass without comment, without that look.

And yet your most repeated gesture was to hold out your hand to me,
    as if ready for the next round of dancing, the open palm an invitation.

Even on your last day, Tina, the hand was eloquent as fate, though I
    hadn't paused to examine the lines that I never could decipher.

In the high humid heat of the August night, I lie naked on the bed,
    my body aching for your cooling touch that would set us on fire.

And in my dream, so chaotic but so lucid and filled with logic's anxiety,
    I thought I had lost you, but still asleep, woke first to your touch—

your arm was thin, for you had been sick, but then I heard you speak
    in that clear strong bell of a voice, of how you had been cured

in London, of all places, and then, so beautiful, I saw you lie down beside me
    and, like Milton and his sainted wife, I cried out for joy and woke to loss.

Such a happy dream and so cruel to be a dream when all I want is you.
    I struggled out of bed—it is earliest light—to come downstairs to write,

and even that random rhyme, Tina, says it all, in this world of meaning
    that traps me in significances that I cannot understand and don't want to.

The early morning sun angling through the black walnut trees
    illumines the mist like a pillar of moist light in some dream vision.

Drops of water fall from leaves as the heavy dew sits on the grass upright.
    Already the day's chirruping sounds are rising and falling like a wind of sound,

and the freshest hour of the day is upon us, as if paused and poised before
    the sun rises above the trees and streams into this hidden world, flooding it with time.

Despite everything we know and experience, each day begins as if a newborn
    opening its eyes for the first time, unfocused, on a wonder, a new world.

I am not going to contrast all this with that other world of sorrow, it is too
    familiar a gesture, so much beside the point when life is simply life.

I am not looking for consolation either, certainly not here, not now.
    I am thinking of you, Tina, and looking for you in the one place I find you.

Today is the day that what I wrote for you will be sung by a choir.
    Not the choir of birds that sings of you every morning at dawn,

but people this time, whose voices will carry my love for you.
    Will they know what they are doing, in celebrating you in music?

I think so. How else explain the notes I receive about you from others?
    Just yesterday, and this morning, two dear friends sent remembrances.

Will this ever end? It's not as silly a question as it might seem.
    Time puts an end to everything, everything that time can end.

When I listen tonight, transported to your realm of finer waves and particles,
    I will slough off the past and turn my back on all futures.

I will join the singers in their song, the song of you, Tina,
    which never falls silent and never will as long as song sounds.

It has been a year and a month and an eternity, but in each
    of the last four days I have heard from people inspired by you.

I thought you were dead. Yet last night, the choir—
    hardly angels, I expect—sang you alive, back into being.

I thought you were alive—so present was your presence.
    I was Orpheus in the Underworld, Aeneas in Tartarus, Dante in Hell.

Who were you? No one anyone ever knew before or since.
    Why mythologize? There's no need for any further resonance.

Every word sung, every string struck or note blown was
    all in all, a vibration of the air we all breathed in together.

Tina, those in the audience who knew you, knew what was going on,
    but we were all powerless to affect it, as it affected us.

We rarely cried alone. It was always a shared suffering, either
      for others or for the other. Like your earrings, drops of opal, or

your necklace, adorned with opal fire—now hidden away in a column—
      your tears were an ornament to me of your spirit, your spirit's spirit.

Now when I weep, I am alone, and weep for being alone, without
      the mingled tears, the wet salt of grief and passion that melts difference.

You taught me to cry as a man should. How am I to teach others?
      Do I stand in front of our house and simply weep for what the world is?

Already people passing by lower their heads as if remembering a distant dream.
      There's no need to embellish anything at this point, it's all so clear.

That smile that lit up your face, Tina, balanced the world, and
      though bound to this life, you laughed the laugh of the free.

There is a holy day each month, O Master, and it does not belong to you.
      Every other day belongs to you. But this day, today, is set apart as if a blank

on a calendar. How to mark this day, which has marked me? Do I celebrate it?
      Is this a day to let go of my suffering, to send it away like a scapegoat?

If so, it is an animal bound to return, to find its way back to my fold.
      But tell me, Master, should I celebrate death as a freedom?

I, who am not free—what can I know about it but what I hope?
      Can I ever be free of debt, who owe everything to others?

Even this day I'm indebted to you for bringing me back to what is most so,
      the loosening and untying of a knot, a rope shapeless and limp.

Master, I am waiting for you to tell me what to do, where to go,
      as I stand at this crossroads, every sign reading "Tina."

It struck me as odd, in the dream, that I would visit your grave
    as I do daily, but return to find you at home as before, as if

nothing really had changed. How could it be? How can it be?
    These August days seem to go on forever, like a continuo.

It's all a matter of circulation, a cycling through the rhythms of the day.
    It takes something savage to cut across this, to unbend the iron hoop.

We specialize in savagery, the front page a testimony to our prowess.
    Do not tell me time heals. It, too, is savage and has savaged all I love.

The grave diggers have misplaced your footstone, placing it where I will lie.
    They have done us a favor, intuiting, as it were, the lie of the land.

I will have to correct them, Tina, for propriety, but we can smile at it,
    a private joke. When I come back from the cemetery, I'll tell you how it went.

My life is bittersweet. You the sweetness, I the bitterness.
    Sweet and sour are like oil and water. Try as hard as you might

they will not mix but retain their separateness in solution, undissolved.
    The hard green ball encasing the black walnut is indigestible.

Even the squirrels gnaw it away to get at the hard shell protecting the nut.
    The sweet kernel is very small within the bitter sheath containing it.

I wish life were a matter of analogy, something you could figure out.
    It turns out to be the other way around: life makes analogies of itself.

If I could live inside out, I would come close to whatever we call the truth.
    But the walnut grows within its shell, and water will never float on oil.

Just for a moment, I wish we could exchange lives, Tina, so I would
    know what my life is and what your death is, or isn't.

I am not the first to have sung you, all your life people praised you.
  And I am not the only one to have raised songs after you died.

If I had died first, you would not have these remembrances for your own,
  I would have carried them away in my heart, leaving silence behind.

When I am done singing, the songs will live and they will remember us
  as elderly parents around whom many things collected and many stories.

To live an entire life, with all the pulsations, day and night, the millions of thoughts,
  and to have it distilled down to a few stories, anecdotes, a few scraps.

The parents die and the family home must be sold, the personal property disbursed.
  So much is thrown away or put into boxes that someone else will throw away.

One day our poems will be sad, Tina, for they will have to sort out our lives,
  and in their turn determine what will be passed along and what left behind.

GHAZAL 90

Grief is a road I travel. It is not something that happens, not a thing.
  When I dreamed the other night that I was dreaming, I was on that road.

Sometimes the road appears to go nowhere, just further on. It is unpaved.
  The road is well worn. There are signs that many others have been this way,

and some tire marks show that a few tried to turn around and go back.
  Perhaps they did. But where did that take them—or, rather, leave them?

When it is dry, the way it has been lately, the dust never quite settles, the gravel loose.
  During a rainy period, which I know will come again, the road softens and congeals.

But mostly I don't notice the road, just the trees lining it and the hills beyond.
  Once, I came to a crossroads, which puzzled me, for there weren't any road signs.

I asked you, then, which way to turn, Tina, thinking you must know the way,
  but you said nothing and just looked at me with a look that disturbs my dreams.

This house keeps expecting you to come back. I can tell by the way
    the silence in the morning and then again in late afternoon holds itself apart.

It will have nothing to do with the goings-on of routine, the clock's version of time.
    Like an old man in his Sunday suit waiting for someone who will not show,

the house refuses to disbelieve its dreams, its long years of experience.
    Often we would go away, sometimes very far, to the other side of the world,

but we always came back, occasionally late at night, startling the house awake.
    It remembers that and, in its patience, is willing to wait a long time.

I told the bees and the smaller animals and even the plants that you were gone,
    but I couldn't bring myself to tell the house, to turn it into a place of mourning.

I have to go on living here, after all, so how can I make our home a tomb?
    The house is waiting for you, Tina. Undisturbed, it senses how close you are.

There is a sinking feeling that goes on sinking when there is nothing
    but emptiness below. It is time to die: you start to fall, and keep on falling.

I've been in free fall ever since, hitting ledges and sheer walls on the way down.
    The earth I walk on is an illusion; the people around treat me as one of them,

though sometimes they notice I'm not really there, just passing through, falling.
    How many of them are also falling, I do not know, but I can't be the only one.

Why don't we recognize one another and reach out at least to grasp hands?
    Cautious, I search the eyes of the people I know and those I meet, beseeching.

A turn of the head, a quiet laugh masking a sigh, gives me hope. You, too?
    But I have no words to relinquish the one question that sears my heart.

When it was time to die, Tina, there was no time for me, only this endless space
    through which I sink, praying that it will end and I will be you again.

I know now how Mary and Martha must have felt when Lazarus rose.
  Their hearts were in that tomb, so Jesus resurrected them, too.

It would have been like a lucid dream, awake within a dream,
  and yet not dreaming, not yet believing that the real could be so unreal.

I know how they felt, right up to the moment when Lazarus came forth
  and Jesus wept. But the moment after the moment before, I do not know.

So I weep, at times, for no other reason than that the sun rises and a bird sings.
  My daily round is a sort of tomb, a place I've buried myself in to survive.

Maybe I shouldn't survive. Maybe I've got it all wrong, and I, too, must die.
  I thought I had. At least my life became an afterlife, though not like Lazarus's.

Sometimes at night, lying awake, I rehearse my death, getting a feel for it.
  It's another thing you taught me, Tina, something you mastered and passed along.

There's nobody now between me and death, so I wait for it, counting my days.
  My calendar on the wall, with its pretty pictures, is an actuarial table.

I've even ordered my headstone, so both our names can appear among the dead.
  Those are my people in the cemetery, where I visit to tend your flowers.

Upgathered like a flower you were, so I fill our house with them to remember.
  No, not to remember. You don't remember what you never forget. You don't

need to remember to breathe or contract your heart, you just do, you're just done to.
  Only the flowers show signs of remembrance. They wilt slowly and die.

Perhaps I should plant a cypress, as they used to, for a symbol. But what use
  have I of symbols when the thing symbolized confronts me continuously?

Dear Tina, my life is one long letter to you that's waiting to be posted, waiting
  to be signed and sealed, stamped, then dropped into a box.

GHAZAL 95

Today—this morning—a mist has settled among the trees, whiting out the sky.
    Yesterday, the white orchid lost its flowers and the new buds shriveled up.

The gypsophila in the vase behind your photograph on the glass table is a cloud
    and I have taken to wearing white shirts every day, though some are stained yellow.

As with everything else in my life right now, I do not know where the day is headed
    or whether it goes in a definite direction or just round and around like the clock.

I live in my ignorance as if it were a simple unfurnished room with perhaps
    a jar of flowers and a wooden crate or two for a chair and table.

When I go out I put on a shirt of knowing to hide my ignorance, so as not
    to upset my friends and acquaintances, who prefer me to be myself and no one else.

It is when I am alone, Tina, in my room of not knowing, that I am closest to you,
    as if all the colors surrounding me resolve themselves back to white.

GHAZAL 96

There is a dampness in the autumn air and a smell of things that are leaving.
    In the gray light, green takes on a deeper hue while the other colors are muted.

It is like the soft pedal of a piano pressed to quiet a simple passage of notes.
    It is like those minutes I would spend outside the door listening to you play—

practicing Bach or the music of the Master—not wishing to interrupt, knowing you
    would stop if you knew I was so intent, so moved by the fact of your playing.

I would wait in a quiet transport of joy, as if it were a private concert
    for me, though really it was just an overhearing of your moments of joy.

It was like sharing a secret, even if I never told you how often I waited
    until you stopped or paused, then coming in as if nothing special had happened.

I think you knew, though, as I was always transparent around you, Tina.
    The next piece of music I would hear while walking away, like an accompaniment.

Yesterday I visited the garden we took you to your last month,
    when June was at its height and you were in your steady decline,

steady, as in slow and therefore as if the normal had been redefined
    as the possible in the face of the impossible, with every day just another day.

The place couldn't have been more beautiful back then, but you lent it your beauty.
    It could not have been more melancholy yesterday, in its sere beauty.

I had word that a family member was dying. The garden offered nothing
    beyond what it always has: harmony and the surprising wonder of the hidden.

I suppose I could say the garden was in decline, but nature is a circle
    and moves in circles, encompassing us in its arms as it whirls away.

I have so many images I could offer up, Tina, but I think you would only nod
    as you used to when you fell silent, acknowledging that what is, is true.

At night—in the middle of the night, when my second sleep begins—
    I wake with a phrase on my lips, some fragment of a poem I'm writing.

I vow to remember it but it fades with the morning, as if meant only
    for the night, for that long conversation I've been having with you asleep.

I no longer regret forgetting. It's as important as remembering, for it too is selective.
    This morning it was cold enough for a frost, but nothing was blighted—a warning.

I live among signs, few of which I can decipher before they come to pass.
    I live among passings. Just yesterday, among a gathering of seekers, I knew

some of them would never return, harvested like late fall crops in the fields.
    I think my poems are for them, too, like little fires of stumps in the apple orchards.

When will this all stop, Tina? This to and fro across the frame of day and night?
    I have woven your death into my life, with you as the warp, myself the weft.

When I look at your photograph it isn't your face I see so much as
　　a slope of shoulder, the tendon taut, the collarbone's hollow, a fold of skin.

There isn't anything there I don't know better than mine own body, though it was
　　my body that knew it better than I, for it entailed creaturely knowledge.

This creature—my body—doesn't understand any better than our cats why you're gone.
　　It is tied to a mind and a body of feelings which perplexes it.

I try to explain things to it, but I might as well speak to the cats—as I do—
　　who know what they know and can make neither head nor tail of me.

They blame me for everything that has gone wrong, and I suspect my body does too.
　　When I dreamt of kissing you last night, it was my body calling out to you.

Dear Tina, I don't know that I'm managing all this very well without you.
　　It wasn't supposed to be like this, picking up shards to try to glue together.

O Master, I have many questions to ask you but you're not here to answer them.
　　It is autumn and the leaves fall in gusts, but some, in swirls, fly upwards.

They are like my questions, which fall from me. Perhaps the ground is the answer to the sky.
　　At night I am pinned to my bed. My dreams interrogate me, but do not listen to replies.

There's no use in crying out. No one will hear me. The road is empty. I am not
　　without faith, but it doesn't interest me. I have hope but it's of no account.

That leaves charity. Is that what you offer me, Master? Is that what this is?
　　Your last word was "Why?" It's too big a word for me, so I write these small ones.

Where do they lead? All I know is that I was born and that I will die. Everything
　　in between is as empty as the road at night and as full as the road by day.

There will be those, Tina, who will find fault with me for turning to you like this.
　　But they will not have looked over their shoulder, nor seen far enough ahead.

GHAZAL 101

Every day I ask you to forgive me. There is so much I could have done,
    should have done, if only I were other than who I am or was then.

And yet, that "ought" rhymes with so many other words I harbor in my heart
    that I think my heart understands it otherwise and does not turn away

from the light or the darkness. Like a hawk it gazes into the sun, like a cat the night.
    The heart probes with every beat every corner of myself, from artery to capillary.

I am not careful to justify myself, said the poet, to which I add amen.
    But I mean it in a doubled sense, neither apologia nor excuse: I am what I am.

What the hawk sees, what the cat discerns, carries only the weight of the moment.
    What I'm seen to be, by what sees me as I am, was once a blind spot, an optic nerve,

which now is the channel of sight, and of knowing. Remorse is beyond blame.
    And so, Tina, when I ask forgiveness I am asking you to remind me not to forget.

GHAZAL 102

I went back yesterday to visit your colleagues at the Museum.
    You were there, of course, as so many of them spoke of you and even joked

that you were watching as we moved your tapestry frame back to its place
    (there was a retirement party, with photos everywhere, and you in them).

A few people had not seen me since you died, so you had to die all over again.
    And one asked intently if I was OK, and wouldn't believe it when I said yes.

She was right, for she had just lost her father and knew such losses are not OK.
    It was one of those days when everything seemed to be about you, start to finish.

Afterwards, when I walked between rows of trees in the plaza with fountains pulsing,
    it was ghostly to be alone, the moment like a palimpsest of other moments overlaid.

There's so much I don't understand but sense as if caught in the periphery of vision.
    Does it all come clear, Tina, the patterns and the meanings, when you look back?

GHAZAL 103

Today your monument appeared unexpectedly, a simple stone bench and marker.
    "I am Thou, Thou art I" it reads, with your name and mine, for when I'm laid down.

So fresh, so new the cut stone, sparkling in the sunlight, as if stone could be re-made,
    as if your death were something recent, a matter of only a few days or weeks.

But it has been a matter not of days but of hours, the minutes spent mourning.
    Perhaps that is why the stone glistened, each fleck a moment of light.

Now when I visit I can sit by your head as I sometimes did to look into your eyes,
    the silent eyes that said everything worth saying in those final months.

You never closed your eyes, not to anything or anyone, yourself especially.
    In the end, I had to close them for you, a simple gentle sweep of the hand.

I am glad we are joined on our monument, Tina, my name there waiting for
    the day that seems already to have happened, uncanny and familiar.

GHAZAL 104

O Master, the rains came and soaked the land, the wind lashing the bare trees.
    Why such fury? Why not a gentle rain, long and sweet, that washes the earth?

We are in need of peace, who do everything with too much force, lacking patience.
    But you, Master, could be impatient, too, it seemed, like fire or windswept sand.

You knew how to hurt, when pain was called for—or, rather, suffering.
    Suffering never canceled out joy, only pain could do that, constant pain.

Today the weather has changed as if nothing had happened, or could. Cloudless.
    Am I to praise this day or store it up against the next and the next?

I do not want to hoard my regrets but spend them freely, extravagantly.
    But I have no one to spend them on or for, except myself, which does little good.

Dear Tina, when the rain came I thought of that favorite French poet of yours,
    the one you used in teaching me to sing. Let the rain come as it may.

The losses mount and add up but they're really subtractions, each a zero,
    a cipher that leaves you as you were, without—but within, an utter change.

It is November and the trees have given up their leaves in favor of light
    which streams through the woods now like a child let loose to play.

Yesterday, with time to kill before a funeral (must I apologize for the heavy hand?),
    I walked a beach because that is what you would have done, or rather,

I do it now because I carry you within, or perhaps, you carry me, pregnant.
    Waiting to be born, what better place to bide my time but by the waves?

The sea was rough from wind and the sea foam detached and blew along the beach.
    The sun was your sister and you were seldom happier than when playing with her.

At the end of the service, we sang again the last song you ever heard, Tina,
    except for the little song I sang that only the two of us could hear.

"Let the dead bury the dead," said the Master's Master. "Follow me." So.
    I am in need of that healing touch or that word which touches and so heals.

This first snow is a heavy one, as if mourning the end of the season, and so,
    in regret, melts and withdraws, soaking the earth, which later it will lock.

If I were to pray now, what would it be for? Some miraculous turn?
    Pray that I might pray? But I do every day, not with belief but with faith,

faith that the seasons will turn over, that one day brings the day after and the next,
    that I will lie down one day and never rise but go to where my life goes.

I must work backwards, from summer to spring to winter to this fall.
    Then my future will be my past and this moment all the future I need.

Shall we let the living bury the living who have died and yet have not?
    My life borders on paradox, Tina, a land you traveled through before me.

Of late, the kindest people have called on me, but they go away having visited you.
  As a poet put it years ago, the best thing about me was you, and so it remains.

I am the shadow, the shade, that points to what casts the shadow and beyond that,
  the sun, absolute in autonomy, aflame with itself, alive amongst all that darkness.

Today is Thanksgiving Day and for the first time we are alone with it,
  as you had wished, having never grown up with it or grown used to it.

This morning, for a few minutes, it sleeted, the white pebbles bouncing off dry surfaces.
  Just a reminder, I think, that the world does exactly as it wishes, if it wishes.

It is gray but bright, even if everyone says we're living in dark times, getting darker.
  How beneficent it'd be to have the will to do, steadying the world faltering on its axis.

It's been wobbling since you left, Tina, but everyone who visits leaves perplexed
  with your shining sense that the way out is the way in, the way in, out.

There is a pause in the early morning between rising and setting forth,
  a circling back to the dream left in the warm hollow of the bed as if asleep.

But it is not sleeping or abed. It follows me and waits for the moment I hesitate
  before the onrush of day sweeps me up, as if entering a stream of traffic.

There are mornings that if I thought of it I'd go back and kneel by my bed
  and ask it to tell me again that story, so vivid last night it woke me.

I would become a parable to myself, how a man worshiped his dreams till they came good,
  how, when it came to pass, his dream took him by the hand and showed him his fate,

a fate that was neither real nor a dream but a reflection of who he really was and would be.
  I think death must be a mirror we sit before at an angle, watching images pass.

Today is your day, Tina, the one day of every month set aside as if it were a holy day,
  as if the calendar could pause and I join you at the center point of wheeling time.

There are threads of you everywhere I go because they hang off me, barely visible.
    Tug at one and I unravel. But then, every morning, I gather myself together.

I do not mean to suggest by this any legend or ancient myth, much less
    a story in which I place myself at the center, who have no center except,

at these moments, you, around whom I revolve like some planetary system.
    I have learned of the sun and moon and am learning now of the earth.

Do I need to offer an excuse, an apology for marking these days with lines,
    as if scratching the surface of a plate of glass with a diamond-tipped stylus?

I am making prints, the way you used to, one at a time, one-off, not knowing
    what the result will be, experimenting with chance and its near neighbor, luck.

I'm not sure you believed in luck, or not for yourself, who were so unlucky in the end.
    Fate and Necessity were more your style, Tina, though you took a chance with me.

When the mask fell and the friendly face vanished, it lasted but a second:
    what appeared like an apparition was a look of hatred, a face at a window.

The Director would not himself have realized the self-exposure, a self kept
    well-hidden, guarded by charm, such that he would never admit it existed.

But I saw it because it was aimed at me, unmistakable as the twang of a bowstring.
    It came during the pinnacle of your success as you were surrounded by well-wishers.

Later, you weren't surprised, since people had a way of revealing themselves to you
    because you could see motives where others saw manners, the code behind the page.

It was why you took joy in the genuine. The pure is still there despite impurities.
    Refinement isn't something you're born with, it's what fire leaves behind in cooling.

How could you be so guileless, Tina, knowing guile so well? Nobody's fool can only
    exist surrounded by fools of the world, all of whom think themselves wise.

Of those who have come out from shadows of late to bask in the cruel light
    of their victory, the word 'shame' cannot touch them, neither '-ful' nor '-less.'

Shame cannot be modified; it sits unmoved, a stone lodged in cement. It is a judgment.
    Shameful, shameless, it's the same, unlike remorseful, remorseless, helpful, helpless.

How far down does life go? How deep into the earth? At what point does it stop?
    There is a great molten outer core upon which we turn, mantled by unimaginable rock.

If I dig deep enough in my garden, the loam turns to claypan, hard and gray to white.
    For water I must go further, through clay to shale and the underground streams.

I live on the surface, among surfaces, as if my skin were all of who I am.
    And around me, above me, the air and its creatures, whose gods are the clouds.

You would be ashamed, Tina, of our country right now, strip-mined, clear-cut, eroded.
    But you would not be surprised, knowing how fragile, like porcelain, love can be.

I, the man who always carries a knife, have gone under it and now am scarred again.
    Before the cutting, I watched my heart beating on a screen, a pulsating animal.

It wasn't even a hospital, just a surgery, in and out, cut and patch, weirdly painless.
    One way or another, we pay for our mistakes, treating the body as an exterior will.

Why did *your* body betray you? To have treated it right, excepting times you didn't,
    to have inhabited it with grace and surety with that gift of beauty, that clear voice,

your vivacity alone should have carried you like thermals into elegant old age.
    In all our years, but one day in a hospital, your last. Who is to answer for this?

You, so good with languages, were learning Arabic, already speaking it, but when place
    names started showing up on the news, you couldn't continue, mouthing pain.

"What are we doing to ourselves?" is the same question as "What have we done?" You were
    as close to an answer as there is, Tina, not to the question but to the questioner.

I have forgotten what it is like to be content, what some call happiness. Well-being,
    I thought, was sunlight through louvered glass in early morning, the magpies yodeling.

I glimpsed it this morning, or rather, felt it, like when an owl sweeps by at dusk.
    I do not expect it to come back, though I will try to make a home for it if it does.

I know perfectly well where it has gone and why, so there's no need to puzzle.
    I keep returning to this empty house, as if life were still possible and not over.

I feel that way often, in this afterlife, walking the streets with phantoms undead.
    I look daily at my name already carved on our stone bench, and at my plot of ground.

I try to remember what my life was like, to recall the feel of it, its texture and sound.
    I hear nothing but the incidental wind and the rush which is the traffic nearby.

I wonder what will become of our belongings, Tina—not the stuff cluttering the house—
    I mean the longing to be and to be with others to whom we belong.

When I reckon our time by decades, each is a book with beginning, middle, end.
    There are so many chapters, and some so unlikely I have to wonder at the author.

The names of our addresses seem made up: DeKay Road, Amity, Buttermilk Falls,
    Miry Brook, Gage Hill, Big Island, Mt. Glasgow. Even the house we painted and

never moved into, the neighbor telling you about the murder (it would have haunted).
    As in a family saga, characters come and go, while some remain to tell the tale.

It's a fond fiction, of course, so common we're already halfway out the door of attention
    before it's barely begun, knowing, too, how it ends, with a tug at the softened heart.

But it isn't like that, really. We live through times, our time, not knowing any other.
    The days seem cyclical, but they're wheels turning over, vehicular to our lives.

When I stop and think of those decades, Tina, I see you in different guises and places
    but it's always you, ripening toward this present moment, out of time.

Your natal day at the nadir of the year, when every day turns brighter for being longer.
    Shall I make a card to you, as I have always done? Who will receive it?

Today I buy cut flowers, replacing the wilted, for everything is a ritual now. So be it.
    The birds will get extra food, the cats a treat, the mice a reprieve, the deer vigilance.

On this morning always I would bring you coffee in bed, and at night, myself.
    I could be foolish with you bemused, a reluctant muse but willing to serve.

My true audience, I wrote everything for you and waited like a child for notice.
    And now, more than ever, I write for you, to you, steadily, in this deep unknowing.

Last night I listened again to you, O Master, hearing as always what I hadn't heard before.
    Am I right to call upon you? Can I charge you with the task of benevolence?

We were, and are, your wards. Death does not cancel the debt. We are all debtors.
    And what, Tina, do I owe you? And why, when I ask that, do my eyes well?

O Master, the Master of Masters saith, "Watch, lest he come suddenly and find us sleeping."
    This is His day, morning of mornings, but today is also our day, that comes monthly.

I would not be born again, though I would die daily if I could wake from sleep, as in
    those moments when I am seen awhole from a distance that could not be closer.

I know you live in a luminous body, Tina, for I've seen it and—touched—been lit as well.
    How many times have people told me you've come to them in dreams and visions?

The eye does not see, a mere organ of sight. The brain sees, and the mind sees the brain.
    What sees the mind? Here the master of parable makes it clear, darkly. It is the heart.

Nothing is harder, or more hardened, than compassion, the diamond in the Master's heart.
    You would not have truth alone, but would stand for nothing less. Why did you die?

Dear Tina, I write to you from somewhere far away, though every day I travel toward you.
    Will you wait for me? It can't be long, as time is reckoned among stars disastrous.

The year is rounding to its close. Shall we praise it or turn our faces away?
  Snow, encrusted with ice, covers the ground, not a blanket but a hard shell.

So much is fastened to this thin layer of earth, brimming with life even in winter.
  Surely that is reason enough to lift a song or—sotto voce—a private hymn.

How is it that anything lives? Without it there would be no death, so dependent
  is it on life, so fragile, as if hanging by a thread, needing life for its very existence.

Let Death praise the year, for it plants itself in the cold of winter and blooms
  in ice and snow. But our year begins in summer, on the opposite side of the earth.

This, too, is worth praising, that winter is summer, cold heat, snow a gentle rain.
  Death, then, must be life somewhere, even if from where I sit it is bleak and chill.

When I leave here for our southern home and arrive at last, driving past your olive grove,
  you will be there, Tina, waiting to join me in my hymn of sorrow and joy.

Another year breaks upon our shores, a wave that will run up the beach
  and recede as if it never existed, giving way to the next and the next after that.

Where do they come from? To ask where they go seems pointless. The past
  is sucked up in the rising wave. I think you must be where those churning waves begin.

How can a single day make a year turn over? Out the window, morning looks like any
  wintry day begun in cold light, the few clouds mirroring patches of snow on the ground.

There comes a time every day when I travel backwards, as if against the tidal flow
  of my future. Future! Such a grand word for the sordid days coming.

I might as well yell into the wind blowing in off the sea the syllables of myself.
  They will be blown back into my face, back into my mouth to be choked down.

Already I have turned my back to this new year, Tina, for it holds nothing of you,
  and is therefore unblessed and empty, unless you say otherwise.

Words make dark sayings, black upon white, blocking the light and casting shadows.
    How then do words shine? It makes no sense. Sense is not the same as light.

Today, in winter drizzle, the sky is overcast and low. We say gray but it is white
    with translucence, for it is day, and everything I see is reflected light.

Behind the sky, above the lowering clouds, the world blazes with light, as if even
    the space of this little world were infinite and not an atmosphere in constant motion.

Why do we look for what is below or behind, when all we are sits there in plain sight?
    It is our sight that is cloudy, overcast, and if tears are rain, there can be no drought.

There can be no doubt when doubt is a way of life, there can only be certainty or
    nothing at all. To put nothing against all is to forget the 'at,' which is a dynamo in itself.

I would make a parable of all this, if I could, Tina, to reveal and cloak your teaching,
    which was your life as much as your words—which had a light all their own.

There is a soughing wind this morning as day begins. The only other sound is of
    a distant plane, invisible, and now inaudible, and the many birds with their many calls.

This is the first morning back to our house on the volcano. The land is blonde, the forests
    below green and russet, the black shapes in the far fields cattle in random patterns.

Sunrise happened without fanfare in the sky, overcast, but with a full array of clouds.
    Always the world is at war but the world itself seems serene, indifferent to our concerns.

It shouldn't be, of course—though that's a human perspective on what humans have done.
    An animal coughs in the tall grass. No one is alone, even if I say I am alone here.

All this is just a record of a passing life and of a life that passed and drew me after.
    I am trying to imagine what I cannot imagine happening, as I could not have

imagined what did. So I've come back here, Tina, to be with you in another place,
    in what will be another time, even if the one annihilates the other.

What are these depths and declivities, O Master, that I should find myself staring
    down into darkness and shadow with an exhilaration I feel when at great heights?

I am drawn to heights, climbing rock faces, repairing roofs, drawing myself atop a silo.
    I have spent seventy-five days at thirty-thousand feet coming to this land and returning.

But what land is this? Folded, sunk, carved into gorges? Like a well, it beckons.
    It is all at my feet. I have only to walk to descend, to be one with gravel and grass.

It is only dark from above, but still it is a ways down, and how easy is it to ascend?
    I am chary of it. Don't I have better things to do? Mightn't I put it off till tomorrow?

After all, I have been to such places before and I know how I will react once there.
    It's as if I'm already there waiting, perhaps a little rueful but understanding all the same.

And all of this from the restlessness of last night—or rather in the earliest hours of today.
    Perhaps you spoke to me, Tina, and I have forgotten it, while another part of me has not.

O Master, do I know what I am doing? This is another one of your days,
    and I have wandered along a high ridge overgrown with tall golden grass.

Do I go on, straight as before, or should I turn aside and explore the woods below?
    And if I make that choice, is there any turning back? I cannot calculate the future.

It doesn't add up. I get a different value every time I do my sums, so how can I
    cross-check or enter it into a spreadsheet? And if I carry on, will I miss

what I'm looking for? The teachings are clear enough, but how do I apply them when
    nothing else is clear? I suspect my instruments. Is the compass set to true north?

The heart is not a reliable guide, but in the absence of another, how do I not listen?
    And the mind, is that a trustworthy companion? It seems to know everything

while understanding little. Where does that leave me, Tina? Or, where does that lead me?
    Please advise me, as you're beyond reproach, even if what you advise turns out badly.

In the hot dry wind of late afternoon, the gum tree's branches are tossed and whipped about.
 The leaves blown back look wet, catching the light—or like tinsel, they shine so.

You would not credit it if you did not see it. To attend truly to the world is to stop seeing it,
 letting it reveal itself as other than what we suppose, having seen only our seeing.

There's so little we do see for what it is, and I don't have to mention ourselves, the least seen.
 That's a given—or rather, a taking away, a lapse we don't see, like the eye's blind spot.

How seamless the world looks in our creation of it. Only the particulars are disruptive.
 To stop and look has always been dangerous, as myths have been keen to warn us.

Our own hounds will tear us apart, so fatal is even a stumbling upon a clearing in the woods.
 It's so unfair, we say, reading such stories or even the Gospels' parables about justice.

I think it's time, Tina, that we moved out into the world to test this vision by experience.
 Seeing and not seeing were always inscribed on the leaves of the book you wrote.

Death isn't night, death is day. It's when we wake up that we see we've been dreaming.
 But life isn't a dream really, it's a sleep. No one needs to be awake to live.

The dream is just there to keep us asleep. I have so many, my life must be fascinating.
 It's one thing to say I dreamt of you last night—that was real. But now?

It's all the others I think about all day, making plans, spinning scenarios, answering email.
 Just now I spoke to two friends about an event in a few weeks, as if the future existed.

Just another dream. Who cares if it happens? That doesn't make it real now. No, my dreams
 are of what happened, or might have, or what might or might not. There's nothing to it.

It's all so easy. And then the day comes, the real day, the one when we grasp the night.
 We got it all backwards. But it's too late now, the fierce sun blazes on our nakedness.

I didn't mean to write this poem, Tina. It just happened, and now I've said too much to retract.
 Thank God who we are has nothing to do with our poems. Let the poems give thanks.

It is easy to make a mistake in the eyes of the world—we are all mistaken by it—
    and there never will be forgiveness, as judgment is the coin of the realm.

It is harder to make a mistake in our own eyes—only we understand our motives—
    and forgiveness is not needed when excuses will do. We are all so ingenious.

O Master, is this why God exists? When the risen sun burns off the morning mist
    and the landscape opens up again, are we to worship the earth or the sun?

Last night the house shook in high wind and lightning snakes brought the rain.
    I knew I should've felt more afraid than I did, thinking I'll know my fate in due time.

It's another excuse. Never apologize, never explain, say the Marines. No doubt St. Peter
    says the same when we stand at judgment. The naked truth we call it. Such metaphors.

Am I on the verge of another error, Tina? I cannot see my way as I'm in my way. I only
    hope I won't pretend it's all clear in retrospect, that I should have recognized my fate.

I have grown fond of superstition of late, it keeps the mind at bay, straining on its leash.
    Half-truths need only be half-believed, which quarters them at best. That much we can take.

When the door suddenly locked behind me, the third to have done that since you left,
    it was like a game or a joke you play on me, a tease. I had to dismantle it to get in.

If you are locking me out, why have you locked me in? Imagine what you will, a locked door
    is a real thing, a real pain we say, though it isn't anything like pain. It made me laugh.

What's not a laughing matter is when the matter itself is immaterial, and you appear as
    an intuition does, something felt along the heart as true. That sets loose the outraged dogs.

Perhaps I shouldn't taunt them: they can't help what they are, snuffling, scratching, howling.
    I think the cats have gotten under my skin, which comes of having had scores of them.

I have buried so many we have a Potter's Field of them, each with an unmarked stone.
    At sunrise, Tina, I wake to your pole from Yirrkala, hollowed by termites, filled with breath.

Something is coming to an end because something is beginning. It's the same stick,
  it just has two ends. It's the same coin, though I can't make head nor tail of it.

The evening light rakes the landscape, lighting up some hills, and sides of hills, leaving
  others in shadow, waiting for the eclipse. Clouds break up the light, shining.

You look and it changes before you can look again, for the world is turning away from day—
  which is to say, the sun—with night in the wings ready to bring down the curtain.

But first there will be the finale of clouds drenched in red, and the unseen features
  of the land suddenly visible, always there but not seen, not appreciated until too late.

At what point is it too late? Or has it always been so, and we see it in retrospect,
  a news story we keep repeating until we believe it? Until the real news hits us?

Something is beginning, I don't know what. I feel it as the shadow of an ending. We know
  a lot about endings, don't we, Tina? In the beginning is the end is the gospel truth.

The sun is up and in my eyes. I cannot look at it directly, like so much in my life, or
  it would blind me. I give it sidelong looks and then turn to its effect, a visible world.

I keep marking these days as if stages in a journey, but it isn't a journey, not even a trip.
  I just keep going round and round like a horse in harness at a well drawing water.

One year and half of one year. What does that add up to? Time is not numbers, nor is life,
  except as a series of X's and O's, which look more like cancellations than hugs-and-kisses.

I think, therefore I am not. That's time for you, the illusion that there is a thinker of thoughts
  and not the other way around. So I plod on, circling the well, musing on journeys.

But I'm not going nowhere, no how. The track I wear is real and visible to others as a trace
  of what is going on with me, even if I can't see it as a whole at any given point.

Tina, I will stop at noon today, the hour of your death, and feel again the desolation that
  went beyond feeling, went straight into my heart and stayed there. Day is upon us now.

Let us watch him go off into his world. He will forget us at times, but it doesn't matter,
    we have each other and knowing that alone is reason enough for this, this gladness.

I don't know what to call it, not joy, not even happiness—a chancy state at best—no,
    it's something below that, and when we touch it, as now, it might as well be forever.

The big words seem a little clumsy and the little ones, though light on their feet, can't
    keep up in the long run. We're left to go it alone, you and me, swift and sure.

From our vantage, he looks a bit comical, lurching like a drunkard from one situation
    to the next, certain he knows what he's doing, that he isn't drunk, thank you very much.

Let's just hope he doesn't do himself or anyone else any harm. He'll sober up and then
    remember us, abashed, getting a glimpse of himself as callow and needing us.

I tell you, Tina, this can't go on much longer, without us stepping in and taking charge.
    But for now, we can indulge him as spectacle and perhaps learn something from him.

Have I thanked you properly for bringing me here? This house was meant to be what it is.
    Building it, I knew it was for you, and every nail and screw drove home that point.

What a wild time we had of it! Throwing ourselves into the work, as if our lives depended
    on it. Certainly they came to, as the house was the sun to our days, our light and heat.

What is love? After all these years you'd think I could answer that. But even if
    I could it would be better not to. I might as well make up images for the sun.

If I were to say sunrise was a forward flip and sunset a backwards, would it help?
    Does a grain of truth make a pearl of wisdom? No, that's too silly, a mere matter of words.

What's the matter with words? Now we're getting closer to what happens when words
    annihilate one another, like matter and anti-matter, indestructible as pure energy.

Maybe our love is like that, Tina. It certainly began as an explosion, and what might have
    seemed its end, when you left, left traces of a law the universe can't do without.

O Master, I never thought this would come to an end. It hasn't, and it won't. But that
    isn't what I mean. There is no end, there is only the means, an end in itself.

How well you taught us, without our realizing until too late that this, too, would
    never end—a process, a vision, like all the others, of what might be true.

Not the abstraction, truth. We only ever wanted to be in the midst of life, living it
    as though life is all there is, the only thing worth living for, even dying for.

I have no scale with which to measure a death, but there have been some that were
    immeasurable, by which I calculate my days and my worth as a person on this earth.

That, too, speaks of life, as do the planets at dusk, stars at night, the sailing moon
    and scudding clouds that put me in my place as one of them, coexistent with you.

If I have said anything at all, it has been at most a hint, perhaps an invitation or petition.
    Dear Tina, I do not think you have minded this long prayer, for you granted it.

Epilogue

I have been watching this poem and this process—it's all a single endeavor—for a long time
    by your reckoning. For me, it stretches like a canister of film unspooled and laid out.

I see it whole, all at once, even as it rolls away into your future, which I cannot reveal,
    though it holds no surprises, at least not for me. For you, my husband, it will all be new.

Your poem has been your Orphic chant, meant to lead me back again to your upper world,
    but you know now our roles are reversed, and I have guided you out of your underworld.

Excepting when I came to you at first, as you cried out for me—my name echoing in the wide
    chambers of your cavernous grief—I have not succumbed to look you in the face.

The myths, you see, are all true, though mostly mirror images, distorted by gross human wants.
    The gods have not withdrawn, they are among you still. It is you who have turned away.

So now, it is my turn. It is out of love that I do this, setting us both free, that we may know
    a new life. Look at me now, touch my face, even as your fingers fade away, dear Paul.

About the Author

Paul Kane has published six collections of poems and a dozen other books, most recently *Welcome Light* (2016) and *Renga: 100 Poems* (with John Kinsella, 2017). His work appears in journals and anthologies in the US, Australia, and the UK, and has been translated into French, Italian and Chinese. Kane has received a Fulbright award, Guggenheim and NEA Fellowships, grants from the Mellon Foundation, a residency from the Bogliasco Foundation, and an honorary doctorate from La Trobe University for his contribution to Australian culture. He has taught at Yale University and Monash University (Australia), and is currently Professor of English and Environmental Studies at Vassar College. In 1980, he married Tina Kane, a textile conservator who worked at the Metropolitan Museum of Art, and who, after a two-year illness with ALS, died in Australia on July 25, 2015. Kane divides his time between homes in Warwick, NY, and rural Australia.